BUT OCTOPI DON'T SING

by

Li Zhuang

**Purple
Ink Press**

San Diego,
California

Praise for But Octopi Don't Sing

Queering form, Buddhism, the moon, and MBTI tests, Li Zhuang's poems are gorgeous maximalist monsters. They are many-armed, weirdly charming, utterly disarming. In this latest landscape of repression and societal collapse, this deceptively small collection will lift you from complacency and despair, will teach you to "let the most vulnerable/ part of your body decide." After all, what is a monster but that which dares to survive—and to take booming pleasure in it?
   —Chen Chen Author of *Your Emergency Contact Has Experienced an Emergency*

Li Zhuang's But Octopi Don't Sing are poems of self-discovery and, at times, self-defense, but they are also poems of passion, understanding, and hard-won love. Rarely do we encounter a collection with as much energy combined with as much precision, with as much formal inventiveness combined with such vulnerability, as when she asks her titular, three-hearted octopus, "How many hearts do you need / to hold your endless grief?" Her voice is distinctive and her aim true. Zhuang's *But Octopi Don't Sing* is a remarkable debut and marks the arrival of an exciting new poet
   —James Kimbrell Author of *The Law of Truly Large Numbers: Poems*

Li Zhuang's *But Octopi Don't Sing* is at once funny and meditative, unflinchingly personal yet historically resonant. Growing up in China and later studying in the U.S., Zhuang interrogates the complexities of transnational living by placing her speakers in diverse settings, real or imagined: the contemporary U.S. after COVID-19, a temple where her mother prays for her well-being, or the Tang Dynasty court where a famous courtier of Empress Wu Zetian questions her own sexuality. Whether speaking to an octopus or imagining a romance with a quantum lover, Zhuang's lyricism remains strikingly honest, illuminating how the poet—or anyone—might endure social, historical, and political constraints. "I am a river tugged/from both ends," she writes, noting the contradiction in her existence. And with wit: "If you hold your chin high enough,/tears would never fall.//How brilliant it is!/To single-handedly/destroy the waves."
—Weijia Pan, Author of *Motherlands*

But Octopi Don't Sing confronts the fractures of language, diaspora, and family with humor, fury, and grace. Charting the metamorphoses of womanhood, queerness, and migration. Li Zhuang writes from the chasm between two languages,

making their discrepancies shimmer with new life. Many of these poems turn on misreading and mistranslation—on the strange beauty of misunderstanding signs and symbols across cultures. Zhuang transforms this act of "mistaking" into a generative center of imagination, a site where error becomes art, and language bends toward revelation—"Z is my last name zigzagging/ on your wrists./ Bend me backward/ and make me/ an arch/ of language." *But Octopi Don't Sing* is a wonderful, strange chapbook—one in which tenderness has tentacles.
—Shangyang Fang, Author of *Burying the Mountain*

Li-Young Lee, excerpt from "The City In Which I Love You" from The City In Which I Love You. Copyright © 1990 by Li-Young Lee. Reprinted with the permission of The Permissions Company, LLC on behalf of BOA Editions, Ltd., boaeditions.org.

Olga Mexina, excerpt from "Requiem for Alexei Navalny" reprinted with the permission of the poet.

Purple Ink Press
6977 Navajo Road, Unit 414
San Diego, California, 92119
www.purpleinkpress.com

But Octopi Don't Sing / Li Zhuang. -- 1st ed.
ISBN 979-8-9892793-7-1

Cover image by Elyon Liu

For my parents 父母, who gave me life,
and for Dr. Han, who taught me how to hold on to it.

Table of Contents

But Octopi Don't Sing, Octopi Are Unwinged

I

On a desperate afternoon, I watched an octopus in my clay pot for too long and it turned into a brain, its copper-infused blue blood boiling down to crimson, slaughterhouse anger. The price one must pay to come closer to (being) a human. My brain, my mama's brain, my grandmama's brain, tossed and twisted in twelve psychiatrists' hands, soft & tenacious, yet unable to heal. Their intellectual ledges unsmoothened by attacks of waves. My chopsticks picked at the octopus. Wet, glossy, and chewy, the teeth knew not where to begin.

II

When a brain falls, will it swim midair
soft tendrils spread out, flying like a kite
in the spring's soft willow wind? Will it
plummet like a block of tofu, breaking into
a thousand ocean jelly balls, semi-transparent
rainbow-colored, ¥10 per cup childhood bliss
sold outside my primary school's wired gate?

When they suck in water, they grow twice
bigger. The sun-rugged granny beamed at
the pool of jelly eggs as if beholding a den
of chicks, envisioning them growing up after
a fortnight, laying golden eggs beside her hay bed.

I watched the fairy godmother of jelly-ball wonders hover
over her white ceramic basin like the one that still stood
dust-ridden on my grandma's rosewood nightstand
three years after she passed away, her white hand
towel—now shriveled yellow, giving off bitter
scents of ginseng soup and madhouse, bearing
the shape of last time it had been wrung, before
she threw herself out of the window. A free fall—
that summer, our cherries reddened with a rush.

The afternoon sun bounced at the brim of
her porcelain basin where a pool became
an ocean, a thousand red and green and blue
souls, too loose to stick together, too afraid
to hug each other, quivering with their thousand
different pains. A motion inside that could not
stop. I tucked a red one under my tongue
cold and elastic, it would not pop.

III

A-live
Octopus does not fall
Water keeps it afloat
It merely dodges
Phantasmagoric danger
Thrusting backward
Umbrella-speed
Disappearance
Behind the ink.

IV

I am an octopus
paralyzed by my ink
I cannot revive myself
by chewing my own limbs.

V

Dear Octopus,
I'm sorry that last night at Flushing's fish market, I called you
a "squid" twice. A mistake made by a Chinese girl who lived
in the States for too long (but not long enough). These reddit buffoons
called you *an eight-limbed Moloch, soft-bodied, cold-blooded
monster, ink-jerking conjuror, an invasive alien*. Me, a resident
alien, stuck between two countries, both we cannot call home.

VI

So octopus, why is "heart" always
phrased as if it's a singleton?
How many hearts do you need
to hold your endless grief?
Does three ever lose its magic?

When you have forty million
neurons converging at the tips
of your tentacles, what is the difference
between a limb and a brain?

How will you feel if you survive
but lose one limb?
Will your misshapen body squirm—
all the way backward
to where it all begins?

VII

Walking across the old Chinatown
with a blue-ringed octopus cleaving
to my frontal lobe, a blue shard, noctilucent
pain—the last missing piece of my body.

Parable of the Rabbit

My rabbit, Miss Theseus,
won't fetch balls of any size.
Her red eyes follow
their moon-colored curves
to their fated plummets.

White fur undulating like tides
of dandelion in high grass,
my rabbit, a well-positioned
prey, watches golden retrievers
yipping with hot fervor,
chasing after tennis balls
tossed far by their humans—
their repetitive rituals
of long-lost huntsmanship
and wonders about Sisyphus.

With two ears jutting
like unsheathed knives
of permanent sorrow,
my rabbit stands
on its hind legs
like an Athenian
warrior, unarmored,
and refuses to fetch.

Once a Chinese Girl Mistook "Abecedarian" for "Obsidian"

A is for apple, of course
        I learned that   in my bilingual
kindergarten   where I scribbled
      on my notebook   ~~Adam~~
    Eve & Eve.   I repent
       under a linden tree.
B is for Bodhisattva Guanyin,
    who feeds me   Manna
in my sleep.   I keep confusing
    one religion   with another.
C is for certainty.   I kneel down every night
      on my cattail hassock   and pray
        to no particular God.
D is for detonation, destruction, deflection,
    ∞DDDDs my psychiatrist   jots down on her Sunday
          shopping list.
_ is for the erased and unnamed.
        _ast versus West.
  Something I'm taught
      to forget.
F is for f**ked up.
    Which country f**ked up
       my mind more?
    Which direction?
  Up or down?   _ast or West?
G is for Gesus Christ.   I misspell
  his name.   I don't believe him.
I hug my elephant Buddha   and stroke her
    tusks all night. Call her
       M'Lady Ganesha.

JK is the short skirt
                I'll never wear   for your feverish
      high school   manga dream.
Just kidding, honey.   You never know
                          what I'm willing to do
          to myself.
L is for love
      is always for
             love.
M is for mwahaha.   Dance with me M. Ganesha.
   Or is that M. Guevara?   I keep confusing
      one lover   with another.
N is for negation.   Your Honor,
      I solemnly swear that   I'm telling you
          everything   but the truth.
                  So help me God.
O is for oopsy-doopsy. I spilled coffee twice.
                between Gesus's legs.
P is for playboy   playbills I hang up
        in my dingy Columbia dorm.
     A Chinese lesbian Casanova.   *The audacity of that!*
Q is for questions   you can never ask.
     R is for resurrection.   I revive
        after 7 days   in the limpid blue ponds
   of her eyes.   Is the world
        in her semi-transparent irises
                always lighter
                  than mine?
O is for obsidian.
    I changed my mind.
S is for selfish, self-centered, NPD lovers.
       Time to pack up   your pocket-sized Gods
      and *Go Back to China!*   My dark-eyed
   Casanova—You know it's just a persona, right?
      T is for teamwork.
How to operate the ferry of Charon

with one missing rib
and sail backward
to no man's land?
U should lend me a hand.
Will U?
V can do this.
V are second-rate
Vita and Virginia!   Honey, it's time
to give luncheon
to eight colonial representatives
whose silver forks carved   a perfect X
on ancient china.
Where is the demarcation of bodies?
Y is history always so complicated?
Y is our history
so fragmented?
My love, when your hands map
the territories
of my body,
will you plant   your British flag
high in my neck?
Z is my last name zigzagging
on your wrists.
Bend me backward
and make me
an arch
of language.

Ode to Narcissistic Personality Disorder (NPD)

My therapist refused to prescribe me Adderall.
Patients with NPD sometimes exhibit ADHD
tendencies... She lost me halfway through.
All I heard was DDDD, ooooh America
has given me so many big Ds that I've lost my count.
Pocketed with my NPD diagnosis, I asked for academic
accommodations, staring into the eyes of
a lady whose blonde curls and wrinkles curved
in the general direction of understanding.
On my accommodations letter, I get fifteen minutes
more for self-introduction, stirring Li-shaped ice cubes
in icebreakers, a front row seat to catch the lecturers'
saliva, and a follow spot that shines only on me.

One time, I dream of the true *Truman Show*
where every character is me: in the morning,
barista Li smiles at me, *hey, want the usual?*
Matcha latte with two extra shots of honey-ego
& vain-berries, no ice. Alrighty, that'll be $7.
I smile back, *thanks, you are an angel with*
a beautiful jaw! I jump on the C train in strange
unity with a 106 Lis dressed in starched shirts and
loose jeans and I don't say sorry when I step on
a South Hampton version of me who squawks
at me, *Unpleasant-Li.* I talk shit with my black
buddy Li at work and we laugh in the same guttural
coyote peyote laughter only I can make, and I have it
copyrighted. At night I walk back to my apartment,
a skyscraper near Central Park where 520 Lis live
in their small aquarium cubes while I lie in bed
watching TV, thinking how crowded this world is,
and why I feel so alone until I see the new Barbie movie,

that sonofabitch producer plagiarized my idea!

I dream of a movie where a Mongolian warrior escorts
a North Korean princess on her unwilling journey to
marry the Khan. I'm both the warrior and the princess
and the movie ends with me dead in a battle trying to
save me. In the movie, I speak three languages and ride
horses in the goose feather snow of North China plateau.
It's the most romantic version of me yielding to the erotic
power of me. Oh, my NPD diagnosis? I forgot about that
already! Maybe it is just a galaxy of luminescent bacteria
spewing deep sea fireworks on my infected skin!

Self-portrait as an ENFP

Fake
Miss sunshine
People-loving
Puppy untamed
My thoughts are
Swift-swiveling
Swarm of Bees
Stinging
Positivity is
My weapon
& bling-bling
Band-aid
I am a yellow
Typhoon subject
To hormones
& the moon
An exhibitionist
Who exposes
Her belly
Wounds
My love,
Humor me & my
Disenchanted
Peter Pan.
I'm a pink unicorn
Herding a flock
Of white horses.
I entertain my colleagues
With my rainbow
-colored mane
& a waffle cone
Stuck on my forehead.
I change my color
Every minute,
30% for survival

70% for fun.
I glue my eyelashes
With waterproof glitters
So I cry
Sparkly tears
Every night.
I offer you
My playboy
Loyalty, self
-centered empathy,
& my wisdom
Guided by laws
Of randomness.
I run off
My orbits to
Hug other stars
& cause collisions
That kill
The Plesiosaurs.

Crystal Boys in Taipei

I 迎鬼 Ghost-Welcoming

Birds have V-shaped wishbones, so they can fly.
    Men have S-shaped clavicles, unfused, so they cannot fly.
I was born with a V-shaped clavicle, and I still cannot fly. I wondered why
    my parents threw me to a downcast sky. *Scum! You filthy scum!*
I never looked back, finally—a scavenger hovering over Taipei's
    New Park, that marsh kingdom of unlawful
citizenry, vermin-infested dark forest. I swooped down, pecked
    at the young flesh, 18 years old, same as me, rotting silently from the
    inside.

II 施魂 Soul-Offering

Young Dragon Prince, newly minted and quickly dethroned,
    ran from his park kingdom, woke up every night to cuckoos' crying
blood in a dirty motel room, face lit up by zippoed cash, salt-strewn
    hunger and accelerated youth, frenetic dance in vomited plumes,
a heretic paying homage to the full moon and on New Year's Eve, fell
    on piss-stained pavement, hollering *Happy Luny Lunar New Year!*
to pimpish fathers and fatherly pimps, to fairy sons burned out in ancestry trees.

Sons of government officials, army generals, tech supremos and movie moguls,
    Sons of wheat-reapers, meat-cleavers, lumberjacks, and fishmongers.
Sons with V-shaped collarbones, swish swish whistle bones, syph-eaten
    wheezing bones,
    oooh-yeah, lightning-speed bullet bones, crash-landing missile bones.

III 焚衣 Clothes-Burning

Moan, you young birds with your V-shaped curse, moan with Dragon Prince
    and his Phoenix Boy, hearts stabbed near the lotus pond, under a full red moon.
Moan with ribs-broken Mousey, legs-crushed Big Bear, wrist-slashed Wu Min,
    Lieutenant Fu Wei, proud young general-to-be, who broke wild Qinghai horses
unbridled, blatant love court-martialed, found dead with bullet-bashed-open
    skull on the morning of his father's fifty-eighth birthday!
Moan with A-Qing, who got kicked out of school for "immoral sex" in Chemistry
    Lab,

who dreamed of his mother's pale face on the night of the Ghost Festival!
Moan as Death approaches, wildfire bringing down the old Taipei, its dark
    back alleys and holy temples, Sanchong City and Tamsui River!
Burn the Film Studio of Eternal Youth! Burn the Peach Blossom Spring, cozy
    nest
    of old fairies! Burn the whitened tombstones of Eternal Repose Cemetery!
Burn New Park, its breadfruit, green coral and coconut trees, hungry eyes burning
    in search behind tall palm fronds, red lilies burning like pierced, wriggling
    hearts.

IV 讥日 Sun-Mocking

God, your bastard son, in one desperate afternoon,
    pushed the setting sun off the cliff, a lighthouse
      in my loin, I harvest men and bait their desolation.

God, your bird son daily offers my V-shaped cure. My armpits are sour,
    my sockets wet, I lay bare my darkest secrets for your meagre
      blessings. I am a thousand deaths blooming beneath a purple sky.

God, your son every night spits red moon flowers into broken white
    porcelain, until one morning, drenched in yellow fluids and fevered
      love, I kneel in the center of a forest and pray to a seedless pinecone.

V 魄兮归来 Returning
Autumn is the season
for migration. Behold the thousand
Vs fluttering beneath a death-laden sky

Eternal Peach Blossom Springs   Moan As Death Approaches
Film Studio of Eternal Repose   Cemetery of Accelerated Youth
Old New Park Burners   Lighthouse King Fishers
Every Night Spit Red Moon   Cockoos Cockoo Coo Coo
Fire in the Chemistry Lab   Faces at the Ghost Festival
Why Can't Fly   Where We Hide
Pimpish Curse   Motherly Cure
Bulletbone   Pinecone
Mousey   Phoenix
Rotting   Dancing
Wingless
Wish
We

I Once Argued with My Mom Over the Best Place to Commit Suicide & Our Disagreement Stretched into Three Starless Nights

and I thought of that innocent summer of my eight-year-old birthday
Under the golden grandeur of the Hasedera Temple
I watched a firefly become incense, burning itself
to ashes and wondered how a being lost
its justification for living
in front of Kannon
the Bodhisattva
of Mercy

Tugging River (拔河)

My grandmother became mentally ill after the Cultural Revolution and in the past twenty years of her life, she became Emily Dickinson, locking herself in her tiny bedroom at the attic. Instead of writing poetry, she wrote five big tomes of diary. When she passed away, Mom burned them all and kept everything else.

The first time my grandma
visited me in my dream,
she had passed away
for 4 months and 23 days.

*Remember that time your mama
told you that she was off work
and had to bike all over town
to search for me and saw me dancing
naked on your grandpapa's tomb? She lied.
Your mama is a liar.*

Mama tells me this story almost every morning
amid her chopping of scallions, mushrooms
tofu cubes, coriander leaves, and garlic.
*I was 16 when your grandpa passed away.
Your grandma sucked the life out of him.
She sucked the life out of this family.*
I watch scallion bits swirling around
two poached eggs in my ramen soup.
What she means is: Don't be a sucker.

God is a cruel giver.
My ex-girlfriend once told me,
as she sucked the plum juice
from my fingertips. *He never asked.
Stop being a giver,* she said.
Stop.

Are you a sucker or a giver?
I asked my grandma
The second time she visited me.
We sat under a giant cherry tree
with golden leaves that never shed
and watched God play
whack-a-mole with a gourd.
She threw a handful of cherry pits at me.
Sweet-landing on my skin, they shattered
into silvery laughter.

Mama once told me,
Your papa and I were abandoned young.
I'm so glad that we found each other.
We are two bitter melons on the same vine.
I laughed, wondering
if I'm the third.

Once your grandpa almost died
of hepatitis, your grandma saved him.
That was why he married her. Mom told me.
A life for a life. I nodded.
It all made sense.

I am a river tugged
from both ends.

An Atheist's Journey to the West

My mom, an atheist her whole life except when
    I got tuberculosis at four, kowtowed to every
Buddha & Bodhisattva in Lotus Temple after
    my flight back to America got canceled for Covid.
Kneeling on the green cattail hassock, palms upward
    toward the heavens, she bent her head till it kissed
the bluestone floor. "Tap tap tap," a mother's gentle knocks
    on the doors of Shakyamuni, Dipamkara, Amitabha
Buddhas of past, present and future. "Tap, tap, tap,"
    a timid attempt to waken the stony deities
to her humble plea of sending her only daughter away
    across the Pacific till their blood ties thin
into a tenuous WeChat line. Her repetitive rituals,
    I first found funny, then followed clumsily.

That night, we kowtowed to thirty candle-lit statues,
    Buddhas sitting virasana on lotus seats, their blue-
and red-faced attendants, angry or tranquil, holding
    Vajras, dharma wheels, swords and shields.
That night, we stood up and knelt too many times
    —limbs folded, back arched, embryo-like.
Bowing to the unseen powers hovering overhead, bowing
    to names thunderous and obscure, bowing to masters,
disciples, and attendants alike, bowing, bowing to the unmoving
    until our foreheads bore the same dented marks
as the knee-scraped cattail hassocks.

I looked up at Guan Yin, the Bodhisattva of Mercy,
    her white vase and her willow branch dipped in
healing water. In her softly arched eyebrows, her dark eyes,
    her tightly pressed lips, I saw my mother, the time-rugged,
pain-mutilated, prostrated, and desperate and Guan Yin,
    the holy, lofty, wish-granting, pain-healing,

thousand-eyed and thousand-armed Goddess—
    how their faces start to become one.
A face of no face; a wish of no wish.

In the grass-ridden courtyard of Lotus Temple
    in the cold evening's pinewood wind,
I burned incenses, bowing to
    the North, South, West, and East:
Holy powers from all directions, Buddhist, Taoist,
    and Christian alike, I pray to you to keep my loved ones safe.
Help me flee from my own country and reach the border
    where once crossed, I will forever be an in-between.
Give me insight and bring me to the other shore.

My mom hummed a nursery rhyme:
    Long, long ago in the East Sea,
a hermit crab wants to break free.
    Shedding her shell, heavy and ugly,
She swims in newfound liberty.
    Years pass and a tear does fall,
for she has lost its cherished hall.
    No longer has she a home to be
a lonely drifter, lost at sea.

Ode to My Watch

"They show as the dial or move as the hands of me, I am the
clock myself."
　　　　—Walt Whitman

7 p.m., I read Neruda's "Ode to a Watch at Night" and stare
at my watch, its jade green dial, hand-engraved, gold-inlaid
family name, its flying tourbillion, a hummingbird who forgets
how to stop its wings from carrying itself upward. A gift from
my father after sitting for years in a ceramic pencil holder with
pennies and dried up bamboo brushes. A gift he gave me
after hitting me so hard that my ears kept ringing for weeks

9:15 a.m., I choose not to go to the hospital but rather let
the midnight buzz-buzzing in my ears merge with the tick
-ticking on my wrist. Because I know that amid everything
the pain, ears ringing, time passing, life is a chronic
disorder. I value the watch though, its grand stand-in
for time my father grants me, a golden shield I wield
each time I feel out of place in a blindingly white
classroom. I flash my wrist, pretending to check the time
but only to check my small reflection on the green dial,
a time portal that transports me back to when I was six—

10 p.m., father was drunk, and I was scared but dragged
my little pillow to the living room where he lay face down
on the shiny wood floor, tucked it under his heavy head,
secretly wished that when he woke up, he'd play Monkey King
with me—let me ride on his shoulders, and brandish my
jingubang before the second sex sunk in. In the vortex
of the minutes and seconds, I see my dark eyes, stubborn
with an angry flame just like his. A flame that helps me
survive 29 years like this time-measuring gadget, wholistic,
accurate, once taken apart, it can never be put back together.

11:12 p.m., violently awake, I stare the swirling blades
of my fan, I feel his fists pelting down on the back of my neck,
my shoulder, my pulled hair, after he read my 16 years' queer
journey laid open on my tatami desk, a frivolous but fatal
mistake and how I hate that double-chinned, red-faced
brute, who could be a corrupt judge, an evil King, a rapist,
a murderer, but also happens to be my father and loves me
in his meagre and self-centered way, who paid for my study
abroad in NYC where I learned the "devious American way,"
and that ticking never stops until I become an old mantel
clock, rusty parts disintegrating with every minute passing
but the core still calling, pushing the hands—*Move forward!*
Move forward! I close my eyes and summon all the Gods
I prayed to when I was six: Buddha, Allah, Jesus, Vishnu,
elephant-headed Ganesha, Bodhisattva Guanyin. Hovering
overhead, they chant together: *Don't look back. Don't look back.*

12:26 a.m. for the first time, I dream that my father is dead,
murdered by my jealous uncle. I collect his ashes in a small
clock locket. My classmates touch its cold surface, and marvel
Li, what a beautiful necklace! I tell them, *it is my father.*
My best friend Chloe, my blonde Florida sister, worries
that my English stops working, gently corrects me:
you meant your father bought it for you right?
I shake my head: dangling from my neck, it is my father.

Death Taxi: A Duplex

On a Sunday morning, my parents got in a taxi toward death,
I watched from our attic window, too anxious to leave.

Too anxious to leave, Mom turned around and waited.
Dad shut the door, "Let's get going! She'll catch us later."

First lesson for a newborn: *She'll catch us* might mean *never
felt so alone*—when a scalpel severs the umbilical cord.

An umbilical cord, once severed, soon becomes a fast-flowing
Yellow River. I, on one side, my parents on the other.

It's comforting to know that on the other side
they will wait for me. First time I wanted to die,

I was 16, so young, so radiant, and so eager to die.
Mom knelt and held my hands, "Don't jump the queue."

Not sure death has a queue, I promised her to wait, patiently
and silently, my parents are in a taxi toward death.

It Was Spring

       & by some miracle, I was still alive.
Our relationship healed
      much faster than the blue peninsulas
        of bruises
    inked in our arms, thighs & upper abdomens.
Our cuts were no longer wet,
    red ellipses mapped out
          a universe
where fingernails and knuckles flashed across—
             blinding tidal tails

Sitting on the sofa, we watched TV and talked about nothing.
The winter Olympics that were boycotted by the West,
"Obviously, it was a power play," said the political commentator,
the weather, the shape of tea leaves in our white ceramic cup
left overnight, unwashed, my long Covid symptoms, the travel
restrictions, our long-due visit to Lingying Temple in Hangzhou
where newlywed couples pray for connubial merriment and mercy.

"You're killing me with honey," I finally accused you.

You were peeling a fuji apple, rather rationally,
    with a pocket knife which,
      at breaking point,
        we had both reached for.

I watched the redness spiraling around your fingers
    loop after loop, swirling—
      a tenuous infinity
        swinging on sharp edge.

The Japanese granny next door hummed her age-old tune again:
    Three years ago, all was well.
    Two years ago, all was well.
    Last year, all was well.

Fanfiction

Shangguan Wan'er was a politician and poet who served under China's only female emperor, Wu Zetian, during the Tang Dynasty. After her grandfather was executed for treason, Shangguan became a servant in Yeting Palace. At the age of 14, she was summoned by Empress Wu, who was impressed by her literary talents. She remained Wu's most trusted aide until Wu's death.

In your fantasy, the gilded eaves of Tang poked at the sun.
> In their shadow, a phoenix rose.
Amid the smoke of burned pepper and orchids,
> the emperor's favorite consort twirled her long sleeves.
Once, in Luo Yang, the moon and the sun shone together:
> In the Celestial Palace, the emperor and his consort shared power.
> (*In reality, you and your girlfriend read the same fanfiction but have different*
> *visions.*)
Your grandfather, the head chancellor, urged the emperor to depose her.
> She killed your grandfather, and hung his head
> > over the golden gate of the imperial city.
In your fantasy, the phoenix soared higher and higher and took over the
> dragon's throne.
She became the first empress of China. You were her court slave in Yeting Palace.
> (*In reality, she is the empress; you are the slave. You pretend that it is the reverse.*)
In your fantasy, she took an interest in you because of a poem you wrote:
> "When golden leaves start to fall on Lake Dongting,
> My heart seeks you, thousands of miles, unending"
Your fingers, swollen from rubbing clothes in winter's well water,
> trembled from the weight of an ink brush.
In your fantasy, you knelt in front of her—you, the granddaughter of a traitor.
> You kowtowed three times and called her the greatest emperor.
> She took you to bed because of your beauty, or your ancestry, or your poetry,
> you were not sure. You closed your eyes and felt the cold
> > of her gems, the rustle of her brocade.
> (In reality, she is taller, but you are a tomboy, so you always top her.)
You imagined her first night serving the emperor, her body vibrating under him.
> He, old enough to be her father.
> She, old enough to be your mother.
She started fingering you gently and you thought of suffocating

her with her phoenix robe. The tips of her
           glistening with your humiliation.
(In reality, you are a sadist pretending to be a masochist.)
She asked whether you wanted to kill her and avenge your grandfather.
      In your heart, you prepared three answers, but none were satisfactory.
                You climbed up and kissed her.
In your fantasy, she took you to bed again and again.
          She told you she loved you and you loved her.
(In reality, you wonder if this relationship is a roleplay.)
You did not answer.
You knew your answers did not matter.
In your fantasy, you drew a map of China on her back.
            Her worn-out shoulder blades,
                wings of an old phoenix.
      Her naked body, a cartography of history.
You start to dream of your grandfather and his blood-stained eyes
            watching over the imperial river.
(In reality, you are sick of cruel bravery, tender malice,
        and calculation behind every act of selflessness.)
In your fantasy, she lay down next to you with a headache and asked you to read to her.
      You recited your favorite poem, written by your grandfather:
        "Silently and gently, the River Luo flows wide,
        On horseback, I canter along its long causeway.
        Magpies soar to the mountain moon at dawn,
        Cicadas buzz in the wild wind of late autumn."
She listened carefully and did not ask you to stop.
In your fantasy, you defied her, disobeying an imperial order—
        a long list of names encircled by her vermillion ink.
Nine dragons of her crown loomed over and above you.
      You kowtowed three times and did not plead for mercy.
(In reality, you know when to let your tears fall—
        from just the right angle and at just the right moment.)
You asked her to not behead you, but rather let you hang yourself
      with white silk from high beams of Yeting Palace.
You told her she had enough blood on her hands.
    and you would not be another stain on her crown.
In your fantasy, for the first time, her body swayed under your power.

She, the heavenly empress. You, her court slave.
(In reality, you are caught in a smokeless battle, and you kneel

tto win.)

She, a murderess in the high palace, spared your life.
She branded your face instead:
your radiant forehead
disfigured
with pine soot ink.
(In reality, you are caught in a string of battles, and she lets you win every time.)
In your fantasy, she still called you beautiful.
She landed her kiss over your marred skin.
In your fantasy, you said out loud that you loved her, and she gazed in terror.
You bent her down and entered her, enjoying her surrender.
(In reality, you have the secret wish to surrender.)
You imagined her hair growing whiter, and her dying in your arms,
but you knew it was not possible.
You start to touch yourself, pretending that your fingers are hers.

Self-questionnaire for A Coward

As bone hugs the ache home, so
I'm vexed to love you, your body
—Li-young Lee

I.

Do you have the guts to watch your partner strip naked, lay bare seven holes around her left nipple?

Can you stop your lips from trembling when you kiss the cigarette burns, the zigzagging worms on her upper thighs, and not dream of getting swallowed by volcanic ashes?

Can your hands melt the frost flowers on her windowpane?

Can you push open a latched window without scaring the nightingale nestled on her sill?

Can you love your partner in a non-inquisitive way?

When you can't find warmth at the tip of a thin moon, can you start a bonfire barehanded?

Can you keep the trembling bud from extinguishing on a cold winter night?

On a cold Brooklyn night, can you not lose faith, and kneel in front of a Cathedral, whose inside crumbles day and night?

When the dark is about to swallow you, can you find the Polaris without a compass?

If your partner's body is the relic of an ancient battle site, can you not visit and leave like a hasty tourist?

Can you keep standing like a dead Huyang tree in the Gobi Desert after a long-lost battle?

Can you pluck her bones from the ashes, and piece them together, a human mosaic, the cruelest kind of jigsaw puzzle?

If her mind is scattered like stardust in ten galaxies, can you weave a giant soul-catcher?

Can you find out the right ways of licking her eyes, her nose bridge, her lips, the soft hair on her chin without making her feel like a chuck steak on a butcher's shelf?

Can you hold her cold and sweaty back with grace?[1]

[1] That grace you have to weave into your daily convo and desperately hold onto, does that exist in this world, where women of color daily have to come through the other end of the chimney, muddy-eyed and muddy-faced? Where is that grace that you are looking for? The grease on your face that costs $30 per ounce, does that shield you from getting pushed toward the coming train on a Monday morning or spitted at during a Saturday night football game? You pretentious prick! Hiding your scars underneath your lace shirt, crying on a No.6 train uptown to see your Upper East Side therapist. You, a Chinese poet, take pride in quoting Lord Byron when teaching The *Tale of Genji* to your white students. Comparing *Crystal Boy* with *Giovanni's Room* in your research paper. A world citizen, collecting stamps on your passport, crossing borders with your frayed suitcase, *have been to so many places in the world with me*, passing customs offices, the blue-jacketed officers' suspicious eyes, their gentle or harsh interrogation, leaving fingerprints on screens of all sizes. Did you find that grace in your nine years of drifting around the world?

Dear Quantum Lover, I Have Nothing

to say, our love is so clichéd—once upon a time
a Chinese lesbian falls for a green-eyed, straight girl,

then the man comes, bulgy pants and khaki boots,
barges into our Giovanni's Room, and finds two stowaway

lice having sex on a dirty bedspread, underdeck a ferry
whose destination is home and happiness takes a dramatic

turn into the bury your gays trope: *why don't you kill
your petit papillon, M. Gallimard, mwahaha?*

You see, nothing enigmatic like the cosmic
equation, the silent calculations burning through

the ridges of your brain: *where is that misplaced digit?*
My dear astrophysicist, you once told me I was the one

who held you back before you broke through the event horizon
and reach the point of singularity, the eternal nothingness,

a photon trapped in a timeless vertex. What I imagined was
a bamboo futon squeezed into a carp-eyehole, spaghettified,

coming out as green noodles. Now, splaying out on our chafed
couch, you grumble about being pushed from the ground state

to the excited state. You, inert like a graphite; me, light-hearted,
a hydrogen molecule, flamboyant to the point of mutual explosion.

Look up from your enigma, my love: our universe, so splendid
and vast, each star burning its blue nuclear fuel, sending off

luminous messengers, till it implodes, a victim of its
inward gravity. My gentle genius, please retreat to your fortress

of parental blessings and earthly bonding, the holy
matrimony, a happily-ever-after firework I refuse to

witness and I'll travel interstellar, a light-headed projectile
with no orbitary obligation, half-blinded after a supernova.

Lessons on ~~Un~~holding (一握の冰)

Back against an open fridge
a cube of ice in my palm
dida, dida, a small puddle at my feet

A cube of ice in my palm
pain digs out a tunnel
the sun seeps in

The sun seeps in
let the melting ice
and my tears fall

in sync—a line of ants
trace the crisscrosses on my palm
searching for the origin of

rivers—an ice cube melting
in my palm. My feelings—vermin
scattering into hiding

when the sun seeps in
I stare at her naked back
under white sheets

and wonder about
hastily reddened dates
that fall too early

In times of despair,
learn to hold a cube of ice in my palm,
another one tucked under my tongue

背靠着冰箱
手心握着一块儿冰
嘀嗒 嘀嗒 身下一汪小水洼

手心握着一块儿冰
痛在手心凿出一条通道
光从缝隙透过来

光从缝隙透过来
让冰融化的水滴
和眼里落下的泪

同频 一行蚂蚁
正循着你的掌心
在寻找江河的源头

手心握着一块儿冰
不见光的
蝼蚁般的心情

光从缝隙透过来
赤裸着身子裹着白床单
对着那个背影

想起了早熟
的枣子
自然早落

学会在绝望的时候
手心紧握一块儿冰
舌儿下藏一块儿冰

Survival Lessons

Li, let me teach you a simple trick:

If you hold your chin high enough,
tears would never fall.

How brilliant it is!
To single-handedly
destroy the waves.
This time let the swelling
heat, the salty attacks
on your lashed shores
no longer dependent
on two cosmic bodies
& their lofty orbits
but the arch of your neck
the bowstring tremolo
in your throat

This time, let the most vulnerable
part of your body decide.

Li, let the tide recede.

《Notes》

"Crystal Boys in Taipei" is inspired by 《孽子》 *Crystal Boys*, a novel written by Pai Hsien-Yung, translated into English by Howard Goldblatt in 1989. The names of individuals and locations are drawn from Goldblatt's translation, with a single exception—the name "A Xiong" was changed to "Big Bear," shifting from a phonetic translation to a meaning-based one.

The tanka in "It Was Spring" is inspired by "昨年は、何も無かった。一昨年は、何も無かった。その前のとしも、何も無かった" in *The Setting Sun*, written by Osamu Dazai, translated by Donald Keene in 1956.

The poem "Fan Fiction" is inspired by the lesbian fan fiction 《上官婉儿GL》, written by 废死 (Faith) and first posted on the Chinese online forum Tian Ya in 2008. Its historical context draws on 《新唐书》 New Book of Tang and 《旧唐书》 Old Book of Tang.
"When golden leaves start to fall on Lake Dongting, /My heart seeks you, thousands of miles, unending" is translated from "叶下洞庭初，思君万里馀" in "彩书怨" "Bitterness on Colored Letter" by Shangguan Wan'er.
"Silently and gently, the River Luo flows wide/ On horseback, I canter along its long causeway/ Magpies soar towards the mountain moon at dawn/ Cicadas buzz in the wild wind of late autumn" is translated from "脉脉广川流，驱马历长洲。鹊飞山月曙，蝉噪野风秋。" in "入朝洛堤步月" "Moonlit Walk along Luo Causeway before Attending the Imperial Court" by Shangguan Yi.

The title "An Atheist's Journey to the West" is derived from 《西游记》 Journey to the West, a Ming-dynasty Chinese novel attributed to Wu Cheng'en.

«Acknowledgements»

Grateful acknowledgment is made to the editors of the following journals, who first published versions of those poems, some in slightly altered versions.
South Atlantic Review: "But Octopi Don't Sing, Octopi Are Unwinged" (Winner of SAMLA 2025 Graduate Student Creative Writing Award)
Georgia Review: "Once a Chinese Lesbian Mistook 'Abecedarian' for Obsidian'" (Finalist for 2025 Loraine Williams Poetry Prize)
Grist: A Journal of the Literary Arts: "Crystal Boys in Taipei" (Runner-up for Grist's 2025 ProForma contest)
Tender Masculinity Folio, Purple Ink Press: "It Was Spring" (Nominated for Pushcart Prize and Best of Net Anthology) and "Survival Lessons"
The Common, A Special Folio on China after 2008: "Fanfiction"
Pleiades: "Ode to My Watch" under a different name.
Denver Quarterly: "Parable of the Rabbit"

I am deeply grateful to the chief editor, Yael Valencia Aldana, and poetry editor, Gabe Ferwalt, at Purple Ink Press for placing their trust in my work. Your editorial suggestions made me feel seen. Thank you to Chen Chen for selecting my work in the chapbook contest. To Shangyang Fang and Weijia Pan, thank you for writing such gorgeous blurbs for my book. To James Kimbrell, who once told me, "As poets, we are prone to songs," thank you for being a lighthouse for my poetry journey. Thank you to the professors who have shown me such kindness, and each of you have taught me something about capturing beauty in words: Robert Olen Butler, Barbara Hamby, David Kirby, Jude Marr, Virgil Suárez, Cy. Weise, Lamar Wilson. To my dissertation committee at Florida State University: my adviser Ravi Howard, Diane Roberts, Elizabeth Stuckey-French, Robert Stilling, and Lisa Wakamiya, thank you for the great support you have shown me throughout my PhD journey.

To Chloe Rodriguez, my blonde Florida sister, who generates poetry like a whirlwind, thank you for your friendship. To Esther Okonkwo, thank you for leading the way and supporting me during the hard days. To Olga Mexina for teaching me line-breaks and four temperaments of poetry. To Nicholas Goodly and Hikari Miya for bringing octopus poems to Kirby's workshop, which inspired the titular poem of this book. My love and thanks go to the following people who have given me poetry advice at different stages of my life:

Gbenga Adesina, Ifeoluwa Ayandele, Yusuf Akman, Mary Jo Bang, Sarah Destin, Savana Ford, Joan Kwon Glass, Sáanii Gonzales, Jinge Ginny Li, Gerald Maa, Hera Naguib, Vi Khi Nao, Cleo Qian, Forest Rapier, Huma Sheikh, Njahla Stanley, William (Bill) Wadsworth, and John Yau.

I have always been interested in cross-disciplinary collaboration. Thank you to the illustrator Elyon Liu for bringing the octopus to life for my cover design, and to the sound artist Van Orhari, who creates stunning soundtracks for my poems.

To all the queer writers who inspired me, Jericho Brown, Mary Jean Chan, Franny Choi, Eileen Myles, Pai Hsien-yung, Richard Siken, Paul Tran, Ocean Vuong and many, many more, who not only survive but flourish and bring beauty to this world, I salute you from afar.

To my rabbit, who is five years old now and whose stubbornness inspired the poem "Parable of the Rabbit," I love you.

To my readers, thank you for opening this book. If every poem is a mirror, what do you see? And please do not forget: L is for love, is always, always for love.

37